Interest Rate Modeling and the Risk Premiums in Interest Rate Swaps

The Research Foundation of AIMR and Blackwell Series in Finance

Robert Brooks, CFA

Interest Rate Modeling and the Risk Premiums in Interest Rate Swaps

The Research Foundation of
The Institute of Chartered Financial Analysts

Mission

*T*he Research Foundation's mission is to identify, fund, and publish research that is relevant to the AIMR Global Body of Knowledge and useful for AIMR member investment practitioners and investors.

Foreword

In his 1985 presidential address to the American Finance Association, entitled "Of Financial Innovations and Excesses," James Van Horne outlined the differences between success and failure for any new product or service introduced into the capital markets. A genuine innovation, Van Horne noted, "must make the markets more efficient in an operational sense [or] more complete." Conversely, he defined financial excesses as "things labeled financial innovations [that] have little or no substance when we peel away the veneer, other than to their promoters." From success stories such as zero-coupon bonds and asset securitization programs to ill-fated ventures such as unbundled stock units, the past 20 years of market history have been witness to an abundance of both innovation and excess.

Few would question placing interest rate swaps in the innovation category. Indeed, the swap market has risen from its origins in the early 1980s to a point at which the outstanding notional principal is now counted in the tens of trillions of dollars. Furthermore, the swap product is truly global, with end users frequently demanding cash flows denominated in any of several different nondollar currencies. As summarized in *Interest Rate and Currency Swaps: A Tutorial*, a 1995 Research Foundation monograph, the fundamental reason for this rapid acceptance is that swap contracts provide an efficient way for corporations to mitigate their unwanted exposures to often-volatile movements in interest rates. Put more simply, swaps have become extraordinarily popular because they help companies solve problems cheaply and quickly.

The marketing effort that accompanied the introduction of swap contracts is now several years old and, one would have to concede, has done a remarkable job of acquainting potential customers with the product's myriad benefits. Furthermore, recent trading debacles (e.g., Procter & Gamble, Barings Bank, Bank of New England) have made financial market participants acutely aware of two of the more prominent risks involved with these contracts: price risk and default risk. In this monograph, Robert Brooks documents another cost of using swaps that heretofore has received little attention, namely, the possibility that some end users of these arrangements are consistently paying more than others. An interesting aspect of this finding is that swaps, which are simply packages of forward contracts, require no explicit front-end premium payment, so establishing this result requires a more subtle approach than simply comparing market prices with theoretical values.

Brooks' argument goes something like this: The plain vanilla form of interest rate swap requires counterparties to exchange cash flows on a periodic basis, with one of those payments tied to a fixed interest rate and the other adjusted to changes in a variable reference rate (e.g., the London Interbank Offered Rate). Thus, at the time the swap is originated, the uncertainty over future rate conditions means that neither end user—the one making the fixed-rate payment or the one receiving it—knows exactly whether the cash exchanges will balance out over the life of the agreement. Standard textbook treatments of these contracts often argue that they are zero-sum games, meaning that the fixed rate is negotiated so as to be an average of the sequence of future variable rates that is expected at the time of the initial negotiation. What if, however, supply and demand conditions dictate otherwise? We know, for example, that five out of six corporate users of swaps choose the pay-fixed side of the deal. So, is it possible that these participants consistently commit to a series of fixed-rate payments that end up being larger than the floating-rate receipts?

Brooks documents that such is indeed the case. He interprets this result as being consistent with the existence of a significant risk premium in the swap market, defined as the difference between the current swap rate and an average of the expected future variable rates. In the process of developing his empirical analysis, Brooks also provides us with another valuable service. Specifically, his work includes a user-friendly survey of the more prominent theories and equilibrium models of the interest rate term structure, with a special primer on the notion of arbitrage-free modeling in finance. Even those readers with no direct involvement in the swap market are likely to find this section of Brooks' work to be quite useful.

Producing compelling research about derivatives contracting is always subject to two difficulties. First, the topic tends to be challenging quantitatively for those without day-to-day exposure to these products. Second, because derivatives are often traded in nonpublic venues, the kinds of data necessary to deduce the market's behavioral fingerprints are often difficult to obtain. Brooks has been able to traverse both of these hurdles, and the result is a study that helps to establish a solid technical foundation for understanding these important instruments. This monograph is interesting and useful, and the Research Foundation is pleased to be able to publish it for your enjoyment.

Keith C. Brown, CFA

Interest Rate Modeling and the Risk Premiums in Interest Rate Swaps

The focus of this research is on improving understanding of the consequences of using interest rate swap contracts, as well as related contracts. Interest rate swaps are widely believed to be basically a "zero-sum proposition," meaning that sometimes you win and sometimes you lose.[1] That is, over long periods of time, the impact of interest rate changes nets out. Thus, entering an interest rate swap does not change the expected return; rather, it changes only the resulting risk profile.

The purpose of this research is to examine, both theoretically and empirically, the expected-return consequences of entering an interest rate swap or other interest rate derivative contract. For example, on average, does a receive-fixed interest rate swap result in net receipts or net payments? If net receipts (as anecdotal evidence suggests), how large are these receipts empirically? That is, what is the historical average dollar return on a receive-fixed, pay-floating interest rate swap? How do the net receipts change for different interest rate swap maturities?

Implications for Practicing Financial Analysts

The research described in this monograph is vitally important for several reasons. First, it will expand the general understanding of interest rate swaps. An investor may be able to use a swap to convert a floating-rate debt to a fixed-rate debt, thus reducing the portfolio's risk profile and increasing the expected return (this result would obviously depend on the investment horizon). Thus, this research will improve investors' ability to analyze the risk–return trade-off involved with interest rate swaps.

Second, financial managers will be better able to assess the benefits and costs of converting floating-rate debt to fixed and vice versa. Barclay and Smith

---

[1] Derivatives, by their very construction, have an overall payout of zero, meaning that if one side loses a certain amount, then the other side gains that amount. In keeping with this view, derivatives are considered zero-sum propositions. In this monograph, we focus on only one side: the receive-fixed-rate side of an interest rate swap.

(1995) observed that, for the industrial corporate sector between 1974 and 1992, 36.6 percent of corporate debt had a maturity exceeding five years and more than 50 percent had a maturity exceeding three years. In part, this research will help corporate executives evaluate the economic consequences of issuing either long-term fixed-rate debt or floating-rate debt. They will be able to compare the cost of fixing their borrowing rate as opposed to having a floating rate.

Third, security analysts will be better equipped to assess the advantages and disadvantages of a particular corporation's debt policy. The economic costs of decisions related to debt maturity policy are important to stock price performance. Goswami, Noe, and Rebello (1995) reported that the use of debt financing has more than doubled over the past 50 years and the ratio of long-term debt to long-term capital has more than tripled.[2]

Fourth, investment bankers will be better equipped to advise clients regarding the benefits and costs of various debt strategies. For some corporate executives, the idea of issuing floating-rate debt borders on high-stakes gambling. This study may help investment bankers persuade corporate executives that their debt maturity decisions involve economic trade-offs. One objective is to help quantify the historical cost of issuing fixed- rather than floating-rate debt.

Fifth, based on empirical evidence presented in this study, interest rate swap dealers can examine the cost of running a completely hedged book. Perhaps over the long run, being slightly long the bond market (receiving fixed) might prove very beneficial.

In the next section, we review the theoretical underpinnings of interest rate contingent claims pricing. Specifically, we survey the various term structure theories and review general equilibrium term structure models. We develop the notion of arbitrage-free modeling and apply it to interest rate swaps. After examining in detail various arbitrage-free interest rate models, we contrast pricing interest rate swaps with actually applying them in interest rate risk management.

In the third section, we develop an arbitrage-free interest rate model explicitly incorporating a risk premium. We build upon the Black, Derman, and Toy model (1990) using a five-year observation period. We focus on how risk-neutral valuation is distinctly different from assuming unbiased expectations. This section provides the framework for assessing the empirical evidence in the fourth section.

---

[2]This evidence was based on the work of Masulis (1988).

The last section, in which we examine daily Eurodollar futures data from October 21, 1986, through March 29, 1996, is an effort to assess the economic consequences of using interest rate swaps. We found considerable evidence supporting a dissipating risk premium.

Interest Rate Contingent Claims Pricing Models

Interest rate contingent claims models are directly linked to the term structure of interest rates. The term structure of interest rates is the relationship between yield and maturity for similar bonds. Accurately modeling and interpreting the term structure has captured the attention of many people during the years. Models that have been used to value interest rate contingent claims span from a direct application of the standard Black–Scholes option-pricing model to a multivariate simulation with thousands of paths. (For a review of valuation of interest rate swaps, see Brown and Smith 1995.) The model of the term structure that we ultimately adopt is a pragmatic blend of simplicity and realism. The model needs to be logically consistent, but value is placed on simplicity.

Term Structure Theories. Theories about the behavior of the term structure of interest rates date back at least to Fisher (1896). The *unbiased expectations hypothesis* states that forward rates are unbiased predictors of future spot rates. In this study, the difference between the forward rate and the expected future spot rate is defined as a risk premium. The *local expectations hypothesis* states that similar bonds will provide the same expected return over the next period regardless of maturity. Culbertson (1957) argued that supply and demand over different segments of the term structure dictate the equilibrium yield observed. He found evidence that the holding-period returns are different for different maturities. This *market segmentation hypothesis* was further modified by Modigliani and Sutch (1966), who recognized that if nearby yields differ sufficiently, participants will change maturities. This theory became known as the *preferred habitat hypothesis*.

Meiselman (1962), using an error-learning model, affirmed Fisher's unbiased expectations hypothesis based on empirical data. Brooks, Kim, and Livingston (1993), however, challenged the link between error learning and the unbiased expectations hypothesis. They found evidence of error learning but rejected the unbiased expectations hypothesis. Hicks (1946) asserted that because of a liquidity premium, forward rates should be biased high.

Most prior studies have documented that forward rates are biased predictors of future spot rates (see, for example, Brooks, Levy, and Livingston 1995; Levy and Brooks 1989; and Fama (1976a, 1976b, 1984a, 1984b). Engle and Ng

(1993) applied a factor ARCH (autoregressive conditional heteroscedasticity) model to U.S. Treasury bills and found that the premium embedded in forward rates is a function of interest rate volatility. They concluded,

> Adjusting the forward rate for the volatility-related forward premium can improve its performance as a predictor for [the] future spot rate. Thus, volatility-based premium adjustments are an important ingredient in determining the term structure of interest rates.

Most prior studies focused on U.S. Treasury data and very short maturities. Here, we focus on London Interbank Offered Rate (LIBOR) data and maturities of up to two years. LIBOR is the variable interest rate commonly used in interest rate swaps.

General Equilibrium Term Structure Models. Merton (1974) introduced the idea of a general equilibrium term structure model by assuming that zero-coupon bonds follow a specific stochastic process. Since Merton's work, many authors have extended the idea of a general equilibrium term structure framework. Vasicek (1977) assumed that the spot interest rate follows a diffusion process. Dothan (1978) assumed that the spot interest rate follows a geometric Wiener process. Richard (1978) focused on inflation risk by modeling the real rate and the inflation rate. Brennan and Schwartz (1977, 1979) introduced a term structure model based on a stochastic short rate and a stochastic long rate.

Langetieg (1980) used a multivariate stochastic process to model the term structure. Cox, Ingersoll, and Ross (1981) reexamined the basic theories of the term structure and found theoretical justification for the local expectations hypothesis. They asserted that holding-period returns for similar bonds with different maturities should be the same. This result, however, hinges on the ability to hedge various maturity bonds costlessly and dynamically.

Rendleman and Bartter (1980) used a binomial setup to model interest rate uncertainty and derive valuation methodologies for interest rate contingent claims. Courtadon (1982) assumed a mean-reverting, proportional model of the short rate and derived various partial differential equations whose boundary conditions drive the resulting valuations. Using a square root process for short rates, Cox, Ingersoll, and Ross (1985b) derived an intertemporal general equilibrium term structure model. Longstaff and Schwartz (1992) assumed a two-factor general equilibrium model based on the short rate and the volatility of the short rate.

Equilibrium models typically start with assumptions regarding the behavior of some basic economic variables. For example, Cox, Ingersoll, and

Ross (1985a,b) assumed a single good economy with linear production opportunities and stochastic development of technology. With this general equilibrium, they derived the stochastic process of interest rates as

$$dr = \kappa(\theta - r)dt + \sigma\sqrt{r}dz ,$$

where θ is the central location or long-term value, r is the current spot rate, κ is the pull parameter that governs the speed at which the spot rate is drawn back to the long-term value, σ is the measure of rate volatility, dt is a small change in time, and dz is the standard one-dimensional Wiener process. Other authors have started with an assumption on the behavior of spot interest rates.

Equilibrium models suffer from several weaknesses. First, the adopted model may not match the current term structure and, hence, will fail to explain observable prices. Second, equilibrium models require an explicit accounting for the current market price of risk. The arbitrage-free approaches are able to use current market prices; thus, they avoid resorting to ascertaining the market price of risk. Current market prices have the market price of risk already embedded in them.

Arbitrage-Free Modeling. Many single-factor models of spot interest rates use standard arbitrage arguments. Each model takes as a requirement the ability to replicate current prices. Typically, the assumption is that a set of zero-coupon bond prices is observable, although one could just as easily start with a set of forward rates or par bond yields. Also, the stochastic variable is usually taken to be the current spot rate (although this condition is not necessary). All of the models take as their continuous time limit a linear stochastic differential equation of the general form (assuming modeling spot rates)

$$dr = \mu (r,t) dt + \sigma (r,t) dz,$$

where $\mu(r,t)$ is the drift term and $\sigma(r,t)$ is the volatility term. The no-arbitrage condition is equivalent to claiming the existence of a probability measure such that the local expectations hypothesis holds. Ritchken (1996) summarized this assertion as follows: ". . . for an arbitrage-free process of bond prices to exist, it must be the case that a probability measure exists such that the local expectations hypothesis holds with respect to that measure." That is, there exists a probability, q, such that the expected future zero-coupon bond value, discounted at the current spot interest rate, is equal to the current bond price.

In an effort to explain these models precisely, we introduce highly specific notation. Suppose a given time period is split into intervals of length $t(s)$—that is, time step, expressed as a fraction of a year. A time line with points in time and time steps noted is shown below:

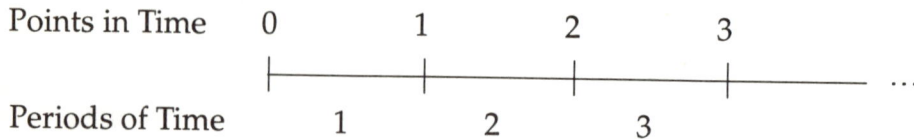

The uncertainty represented by a stochastic process will be modeled with a binomial lattice framework. Let

$P_i^t(T)$ =   a zero-coupon, default-free bond paying \$1.00 at T, observed at t, given that we are at state i

q_i^t =   the risk-neutral probability that rates will rise, observed at t, given state i

$r_i^t(1)$ =   the continuously compounded spot interest rate (one-period rate), observed at t, given state i

$f_i^t(j,k)$ =   the forward rate for periods between j and k $(j < k)$, observed at t, given state i

$F_i^t(j,k)$ =   the forward price for a bond at point in time j, maturing at point in time k, observed at t, given state i

M_i^t =   the value of a money-market account (a deposit earning at the one-period spot rate), observed at t, given state i, starting with \$1.00 at $t = 0$

The value of the money market account is \$1.00 grossed up by the interest earnings in the account, given the particular rates observed. That is,

$$M_i^t = \exp\left[\sum_{j=0}^{t} r_i^j(1)\right].$$

We assume throughout that quoted interest rates are compounded continuously unless otherwise explicitly noted.

With this notation, we know the relationship between forward rates and forward prices (assuming \$1.00 par) is

$$F_i^t(j,k) = \exp[-f_i^t(j,k)\,ts\,(k-j)].$$

Zero-coupon bonds can be expressed in terms of forward rates or forward prices as

$$P_i^t(T) = \exp\left[-ts\sum_{j=0}^{T-1} f_i^t(j,j+1)\right]$$

$$P_i^t(T) = \prod_{j=0}^{T-1} F_i^t(j, j+1).$$

As an example, suppose we observe the following spot rate and forward rates at $t = 0$:

$r_0^0(1)$ =   5.0%

$f_0^0(1,2)$ =   5.25%

$f_0^0(2,3)$ =   5.30%.

Assuming one-year time steps, we compute the zero-coupon bond prices as

$P_0^0(1)$ = $\exp(-0.05) = \$0.9512294$

$P_0^0(2)$ = $\exp(-0.05 - 0.0525) = \$0.9025781$

$P_0^0(3)$ = $\exp(-0.05 - 0.0525 - 0.0530) = \$0.8559871.$

The current single-period forward prices are

$F_0^0(1,2)$ = $\exp(-0.0525) = \$0.948854$

$F_0^0(2,3)$ = $\exp(-0.0530) = \$0.9483800.$

In practice, the zero-coupon prices are typically used as inputs, and then forward rates and forward prices are computed.

At this point, we need a method of introducing uncertainty while making sure that the model does not permit riskless arbitrage. Most practical applications of single-factor models rely on a lattice approach to representing the uncertainty of future rate movements and focus primarily on a binomial tree (two arcs at each node). No unique way exists to represent the up- and down-arcs along with the probabilities of each event; rather, the binomial model can be implemented in multiple ways. To achieve the appropriate limits, the up-jump, down-jump, and probability of the up-jump are expressed as[3]

$$u = \exp\left[\hat{m}(ts) + \sigma\sqrt{ts}\right]$$

$$d = \exp\left[\hat{m}(ts) - \sigma\sqrt{ts}\right]$$

$$p = \frac{1}{2}\left(1 + \frac{\mu - \hat{m}}{\sigma}\sqrt{ts}\right).$$

In the limit, as the time step goes to zero, the parameters will converge to the mean (μ) and standard deviation (σ) for any choice of $\hat{m}$. If we choose $\mu = \hat{m}$, the probability will always be one-half. This choice, however, is strictly

---

[3]We assume here that $\sigma(r,t)$ is of the form $\sigma(t)r$.

arbitrary. Some of the original work on the binomial model assumed $\hat{m} = 0$. (For more details, see Nawalkha and Chambers 1995.)

Figure 1 illustrates the binomial approach to modeling spot rates. Every effort is made to assure that the tree recombines, that is, an up-move followed by a down-move results in the same rate as a down-move followed by an up-move. A nonrecombining tree (called a bushy tree or an exploding tree) quickly becomes unwieldy because the number of observations grows at a rate of 2^n, where n is the number of time steps. A recombining tree grows at a rate of n and, hence, remains tractable.

Figure 1. The Binomial Approach to Modeling Spot Rates

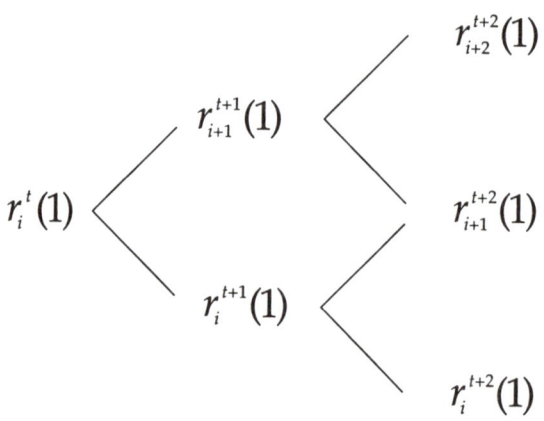

In a binomial setup, the state can be represented by the number of up-moves, denoted here as i. The first arc going up shows i going to $i + 1$ as we move from time t to $t + 1$. Alternatively, the first arc going down shows i staying the same and, hence, implicitly going down. Because this tree is a binomial one, the arc must go either up or down.

Through careful selection of parameters, the spot rate two periods out will be the same whether the path followed went up then down or down then up. At times, however, this procedure is not acceptable (for example, when the security is highly path dependent, such as with some mortgage-backed securities).

A large number of results—the spot rate, forward rates, and forward prices—can be derived with zero-coupon bond prices alone. With zero-coupon bonds, the yield to maturity, $y(n)$, is the rate that solves the following equation:

$$P(n) = \$1.00 \exp[-ny(n)],$$

or

$$y(n) = \frac{\ln[\$1.00/P(n)]}{n}.$$

Using the prices so computed, we have

$$y_0^0(1) = \frac{\ln[\$1.00/\$0.9512294]}{1} = 5.0\%$$

$$y_0^0(2) = \frac{\ln[\$1.00/\$0.9025781]}{2} = 5.125\%$$

$$y_0^0(3) = \frac{\ln[\$1.00/\$0.8559871]}{3} = 5.1833\%.$$

We can also compute the equilibrium swap rates.

Interest Rate Swaps. Interest rate swaps are essentially a portfolio of forward rate agreements. Loosely, the value of a receive-floating, pay-fixed interest rate swap is

$$V_{swap} = NP \sum_{j=0}^{n-1} P_i^t(j+1)\left(\frac{NAD_{j+1}}{NTD}\right)[\tilde{r}_{i,d}^t(j,j+1) - r_{fixed,d}].$$

NP is the notional principal determining the cash amount of the coupon payments. NAD is the number of accrued days in the settlement period, and NTD is the number of total days in the year. The last, bracketed term is the difference between the floating spot rate and some predetermined fixed swap rate. The subscript d denotes discrete compounding. The floating interest rate is unknown.

The current market rate for converting an uncertain future floating rate to a known fixed rate comes from nothing more than a forward rate agreement or futures contract.[4] Hence, the appropriate value of an interest rate swap, V_{swap}, can be found by substituting the forward rate for the floating rate; that is,

$$V_{swap} = NP \sum_{j=0}^{n-1} P_i^t(j+1)\left(\frac{NAD_{j+1}}{NTD}\right)[f_{i,d}^t(j,j+1) - r_{fixed,d}].$$

Although swaps can be structured in a wide variety of ways, typically they are settled in arrears (one period later) on a cash flow basis. Hence, the rates

---

[4]Some well-documented differences exist between forward rates and the rate implied by futures contracts. See, for example, Burghardt and Hoskins (1994, 1995a, 1995b).

used to compute swap payments are discretely compounded. Solving for the fixed rate, $\hat{r}_{fixed,d}$, that makes the current swap value zero gives

$$\hat{r}_{fixed,d} = \frac{\displaystyle\sum_{j=0}^{n-1} P_i^t(j+1)\left(\frac{NAD_{j+1}}{NTD}\right)f_{i,d}^t(j,j+1)}{\displaystyle\sum_{j=0}^{n-1} P_i^t(j+1)\left(\frac{NAD_{j+1}}{NTD}\right)}.$$

The previous data $[r_0^0(1) = 5.0\%,\ f_0^0(1,2) = 5.25\%,\ \text{and}\ f_0^0(2,3) = 5.30\%]$ are converted to annual compounding (typically swap contracts require matching actual interest cash flows, not quoted interest rates). Hence, assuming annual periods, 5.0 percent becomes 5.1271 percent; that is, $\exp(r) - 1 = \exp(0.05) - 1$.[5] The equilibrium fixed swap rates, forward rates, and yield to maturity (based on an annuity), given these data with annual compounding, are presented in Table 1. Thus, the swap curve lies below the annualized forward curve and above the annualized yield to maturity for annuities.

Table 1.   Equilibrium Swap and Forward Rates and Yields to Maturity

Maturity (years)	Swap Rate	Forward Rate	Yield to Maturity
1	5.1271%	5.1271%	5.1271%
2	5.2552	5.3903	5.2132
3	5.3145[a]	5.4430	5.2647

[a]The three-year swap rate is derived as follows:

5.3145% = ($0.9512294 × 5.1271% + $0.9025781 × 5.3903% + $0.8559871 × 5.4430%) / ($0.9512294
        + $0.9025781 + $0.8559871) = 14.4013528/2.7097946.

Review of Arbitrage-Free Models. The economic trade-offs when using interest rate swaps can be assessed only when we introduce uncertainty into the analysis. Several methods have been used to model uncertainty on the term structure. Typically, uncertainty is modeled by a stochastic differential equation.

The Ho and Lee Model. Ho and Lee (1986) provided one of the first arbitrage-free models of the term structure. They described their model as "a relative-pricing model in the sense that we price our contingent claims relative to the observed term structure; we do not endogenize the term structure as Cox, Ingersoll, and Ross [1985b] and Brennan and Schwartz [1977] do."

---

[5]Recall that 1 plus the annual rate must equal the exponential of the continuously compounded rate for a one-year period.

Ho and Lee proposed additive, approximately normally distributed shocks to the term structure. The stochastic differential equation can be expressed as

$$dr = \mu(t)dt + \sigma dz.$$

The mean of the spot price process, $\mu(t)$, is selected so as to match exactly the current term structure. Note that the volatility parameter, σ, is in absolute terms and is not proportional to rate levels (as it is in most stock price models). Also, the tree automatically recombines because of its additive nature. In a binomial lattice, the up- and down-jumps are expressed, respectively, as

$$r_{i+1}^{t+1}(1) = r_i^t(1) + \mu^t(ts) + \sigma\sqrt{ts}$$

and

$$r_i^{t+1}(1) = r_i^t(1) + \mu^t(ts) - \sigma\sqrt{ts},$$

where μ^t is the drift rate (t denotes a point in time, not μ raised to a power).

One important feature of interest rate models is internal consistency, or the no-arbitrage condition. To explain this feature, we introduce the notion of state claims. In the binomial setup, at each point in time, n, there are $n + 1$ possible states. A state claim is the present value of receiving \$1.00 in a given state at a given point in time (and receiving nothing else at any other state or time).

To be internally consistent, it must be that

$$P_0^0(n) = \sum_{j=0}^{n} SC_j^n,$$

where SC_j^n is the current value of receiving \$1.00 at n, given that state j has occurred. Hence, owning a state claim for each state possible at point in time n pays \$1.00 for sure at n no matter which state ultimately occurs. Thus, the sum of the state claims must equal the current zero-coupon, default-free bond price for a bond maturing at n.

Because q is a risk-neutral probability measure, when $n = 1$, we know that

$$SC_0^1 = P_0^0(1)(1 - q_0^0) \text{ (rates go down)},$$

$$SC_1^1 = P_0^0(1)q_0^0 \text{ (rates go up)};$$

hence,

$$SC_0^1 + SC_1^1 = P_0^0(1)(1 - q_0^0) + P_0^0(1)q_0^0$$
$$= P_0^0(1).$$

When $n > 1$,

$$SC_0^n = SC_0^{n-1} P_0^{n-1}(1)(1 - q_0^{n-1})(\text{rates always down}),$$

$$SC_n^n = SC_{n-1}^{n-1} P_{n-1}^{n-1}(1)q_{n-1}^{n-1} \text{ (rates always up)},$$

$$SC_j^n = SC_j^{n-1} P_j^{n-1}(1)(1 - q_j^{n-1}) + SC_{j-1}^{n-1} P_{j-1}^{n-1}(1)q_{j-1}^{n-1} \text{ (intermediate rates)}.$$

In this analysis, we assumed that the risk-neutral probability is constant at 1/2 and appropriately adjusted the up- and down-jumps (recall that this assumption is arbitrary).

Another way to model the no-arbitrage condition is

$$P_i^t(T) = P_i^t(1)[q_i^t P_{i+1}^{t+1}(T-1) + (1 - q_i^t)P_i^{t+1}(T-1)].$$

An alternative way to express this equation is to introduce relative prices. In the equation below, the prices have been divided by the value of a money-market account. On the left-hand side, the value of the money-market account is \$1.00 (assuming $t = 0$), whereas on the right-hand side, the value of the money-market account is \$1.00 grossed up by the interest paid for one time step $[P_i t(1)]$. Thus, we can express this result as

$$R_i^t(T) = q_i^t R_{i+1}^{t+1}(T-1) + (1 - q_i^t)R_i^{t+1}(T-1).$$

The relative price at T is the expected value (with q probability) of the relative price in the previous period $(T-1)$. Formally, under the q probability measure, the relative price is said to follow a martingale. Remember, however, that q is not the actual probability measure (the actual probability measure is not unique but varies from investor to investor).

The no-arbitrage condition requires that a two-period bond be equal to the discounted expected value of a one-period bond one period from now under a risk-neutral probability measure or that the sum of the state claims equal the initial term structure. The free variable, given the assumption of equally probable up- and down-jumps, is the drift rate, μ^t.

Solving for the appropriate drift term in the previous example, the first-year drift term is 0.255 percent and the second-year drift term is 0.065 percent, assuming an absolute volatility of 0.01.[6] The expected future spot rates, under the risk-neutral probability measure, are 5.255 percent and 5.32 percent, respectively.[7] The expected one-period spot prices are \$0.948854

---

[6]We used the Microsoft Excel (version 5.0) solver routine for these examples.
[7]5.255% = 0.50(6.255%) + 0.50(4.255%), and 5.32% = 0.25(7.32%) + 0.50(5.32%) + 0.25(3.32%).

and $0.948285, respectively. Figure 2 illustrates the first three points in time ($t = 0,1,2$) in the binomial lattice based on the Ho and Lee model.

Figure 2.   Binomial Lattice Based on the Ho and Lee Model

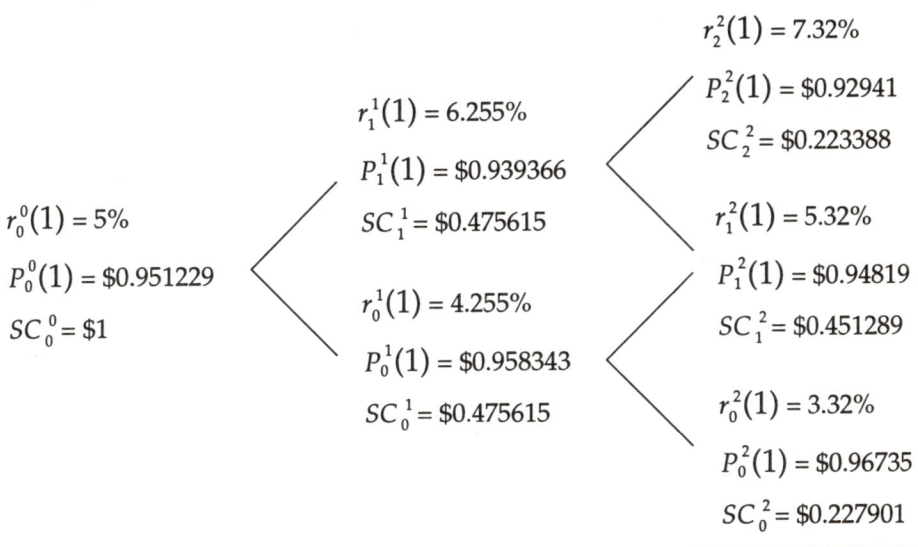

$$r_2^2(1) = 7.32\%$$
$$P_2^2(1) = \$0.92941$$
$$SC_2^2 = \$0.223388$$

$$r_1^1(1) = 6.255\%$$
$$P_1^1(1) = \$0.939366$$
$$SC_1^1 = \$0.475615$$

$$r_1^2(1) = 5.32\%$$
$$P_1^2(1) = \$0.94819$$
$$SC_1^2 = \$0.451289$$

$$r_0^0(1) = 5\%$$
$$P_0^0(1) = \$0.951229$$
$$SC_0^0 = \$1$$

$$r_0^1(1) = 4.255\%$$
$$P_0^1(1) = \$0.958343$$
$$SC_0^1 = \$0.475615$$

$$r_0^2(1) = 3.32\%$$
$$P_0^2(1) = \$0.96735$$
$$SC_0^2 = \$0.227901$$

An alternative way to value swaps is to use caps and floors. Interest rate caps are derivatives that benefit from rising interest rates. They are a portfolio of interest rate call options. Hence, the value of an interest rate cap can be expressed as

$$CAP_0^{\,n} = NP \sum_{\tau=0}^{n-1} \left(\frac{NAD_{\tau+1}}{NTD} \right) \sum_{j=0}^{\tau} SC_j^{\tau} P_j^{\tau}(1) \max[0, r_{j,d}^{\tau}(1) - X_d],$$

where X_d is the strike rate and τ is the point in time when each state is being evaluated. We assume that the cash flows are settled in arrears, or one period later, which explains the one-period discounting represented by $P_j^{\tau}(1)$. For example, assuming discrete cash flows and a 5.3145 percent strike, a three-year cap based on the data from the Ho and Lee method is valued at[8]

$CAP(5.3145\%,3\text{–year}) = 0.475615(0.939366)(0.064548 - 0.053145)$ (Time 1, State 1)
$\qquad + 0.451289(0.94819)(0.054641 - 0.053145)$ (Time 2, State 1)
$\qquad + 0.223388(0.92941)(0.075946 - 0.053145)$ (Time 2, State 2)
$\qquad = 0.005095 + 0.000640 + 0.004734$
$\qquad = 1.0469\%$ of NP.

---

[8] Figure 2 is in continuously compounded rates, and swaps pay based on an annual rate. Hence, at Time 1, State 1, we have 6.4548 percent $= \exp(0.06255) - 1$.

Notice that the value of the cap is the payoff in each state multiplied by the state-claims value (without the day-count adjustment NAD/NTD).

Interest rate floors are derivatives that benefit from falling interest rates. Floors are a portfolio of interest rate put options. Hence, the value of an interest rate floor can be expressed as

$$FLR_0{}^n = NP \sum_{\tau=0}^{n-1} \left(\frac{NAD_{\tau+1}}{NTD}\right) \sum_{j=0}^{\tau} SC_j{}^\tau P_j{}^\tau (1) max[0, X_d - r_{j,d}^\tau (1)].$$

A 5.3145 percent strike, three-year floor based on the data from the Ho and Lee method is valued at

$$
\begin{aligned}
FLR(5.3145\%, 3\text{--year}) &= 1.0(0.951229)(0.053145 - 0.051271) \text{ (Time 0, State 0)}\\
&+ 0.475615(0.95834)(0.053145 - 0.043468) \text{ (Time 1, State 0)}\\
&+ 0.227901(0.96735)(0.053145 - 0.033757) \text{ (Time 2, State 0)}\\
&= 0.001783 + 0.004411 + 0.004274\\
&= 1.0468\% \text{ of } NP.
\end{aligned}
$$

Notice again that the value of the floor is the payoff in each state times the state-claims value. It is not a coincidence that the values of the cap and the floor are equal (ignoring rounding error) when the strike rate is 5.3145 percent. Recall that the three-year swap rate is 5.3145 percent. Thus, one way to value an interest rate swap is as a combination of a cap and a floor with the same strike rate. Specifically, a receive-fixed, pay-floating interest rate swap is equivalent to being long a floor and short a cap. Conversely, a receive-floating, pay-fixed interest rate swap is equivalent to being short a floor and long a cap. Solving for the strike rate that yields a combined value of zero, we have

$$X_d = \frac{\displaystyle\sum_{\tau=0}^{n-1} \left(\frac{NAD_{\tau+1}}{NTD}\right) \sum_{j=0}^{\tau} SC_j{}^\tau P_j{}^\tau (1) r_{j,d}^\tau (1)}{\displaystyle\sum_{\tau=0}^{n-1} \left(\frac{NAD_{\tau+1}}{NTD}\right) \sum_{j=0}^{\tau} SC_j{}^\tau P_j{}^\tau (1)}.$$

The Lognormal Model. The lognormal model assumes that interest rates follow the same stochastic process as stock prices in the Black–Scholes framework. In our notation, the stochastic differential equation can be expressed as

$$dr = \mu(t)rdt + \sigma rdz,$$

or[9]

$$d\ln(r) = \left[\mu(t) - \frac{\sigma}{2}\right] dt + \sigma dz.$$

---

[9]This equivalence can be verified by a direct application of Ito's lemma.

One advantage of this approach is that negative interest rates are not possible. Another advantage is that interest rate volatility is proportional to rate level. Hence, in a high-rate environment, interest rates are more volatile on an absolute basis than they are in a low-rate environment. This relationship appears reasonable based on historical observation.

One disadvantage of this method is that it ignores the strong mean-reverting tendencies of interest rates. The standard deviation is proportional to the level of interest rates but is still independent of time.

The lognormal model implicitly contains assumptions regarding the term structure of volatilities. As will be illustrated with Eurodollar futures (EDF) data, forward rate volatility is not constant across the term structure; rather, it declines. The economic intuition is that current information will affect current rates to a greater degree than longer dated forward rates. What does the current employment number say about three-month interest rates 10 years out? For example, on March 8, 1996 (a day when a high employment number was announced), the March 1997 EDF was up 59 basis points in rate whereas the March 2005 EDF was up only 26 basis points.

Again, the no-arbitrage condition requires that the sum of the state claims equal the observable risk-free zero-coupon bond price. The free variable, given equally probable up- and down-jumps, is the drift rate. In this case, the volatility measure is proportional, and we chose 20 percent (1%/0.05). Because of the lognormality assumption, the up- and down-jumps, respectively, are represented as

$$r_{i+1}^{t+1}(1) = r_i^t(1) \exp[\mu^t(ts) + \sigma\sqrt{ts}]$$

and

$$r_i^{t+1}(1) = r_i^t(1) \exp[\mu^t(ts) - \sigma\sqrt{ts}].$$

The first-year drift term is found to be 2.99463 percent, and the second-year drift term is –0.72527 percent. Note that the expected future spot rates, under the risk-neutral probability measure, are 5.2554 percent for Year 2 and 5.3221 percent for Year 3.[10] The expected one-period spot prices are $0.948854 and $0.94828, respectively. Figure 3 illustrates the first three points in time ($t = 0,1,2$) based on the lognormal model.

Although this rate tree is distinctly different from that generated by the Ho and Lee model, the value of a portfolio that is long a cap and short a floor is zero at the equilibrium swap rate; that is, (recall we used discrete rates)

---

[10] 5.2554% = 0.50(6.2927%) + 0.50(4.2181%), and 5.3221% = 0.25(7.6303%) + 0.50(5.1148%) + 0.25(3.4285%). Recall that a spot rate observed at a point in Time 1 is for Period 2.

$CAP(5.3145\%, \text{3-year}) = 0.475615\,(0.93901)\,(0.064949 - 0.053145)\,(\text{Time 1, State 1})$
$\qquad\qquad\qquad\qquad + 0.22330\,(0.92654)\,(0.079319 - 0.053145)\,(\text{Time 2, State 2})$
$\qquad\qquad\qquad\qquad = 0.005272 + 0.005415$
$\qquad\qquad\qquad\qquad = 1.0687\% \text{ of } NP,$

and

$FLR(5.3145\%, \text{3-year}) = \$1.0\,(0.951229)\,(0.053145 - 0.051271)\,(\text{Time 0, State 0})$
$\qquad\qquad\qquad\qquad + 0.475615\,(0.95870)\,(0.053145 - 0.043083)\,(\text{Time 1, State 0})$
$\qquad\qquad\qquad\qquad + 0.22799\,(0.96630)\,(0.053145 - 0.034880)\,(\text{Time 2, State 0})$
$\qquad\qquad\qquad\qquad + 0.45129\,(0.95014)\,(0.053145 - 0.052479)\,(\text{Time 2, State 1})$
$\qquad\qquad\qquad\qquad = 0.001783 + 0.004588 + 0.004024 + 0.000286$
$\qquad\qquad\qquad\qquad = 1.0681\% \text{ of } NP.$

Figure 3.   Binomial Lattice: Lognormal Model

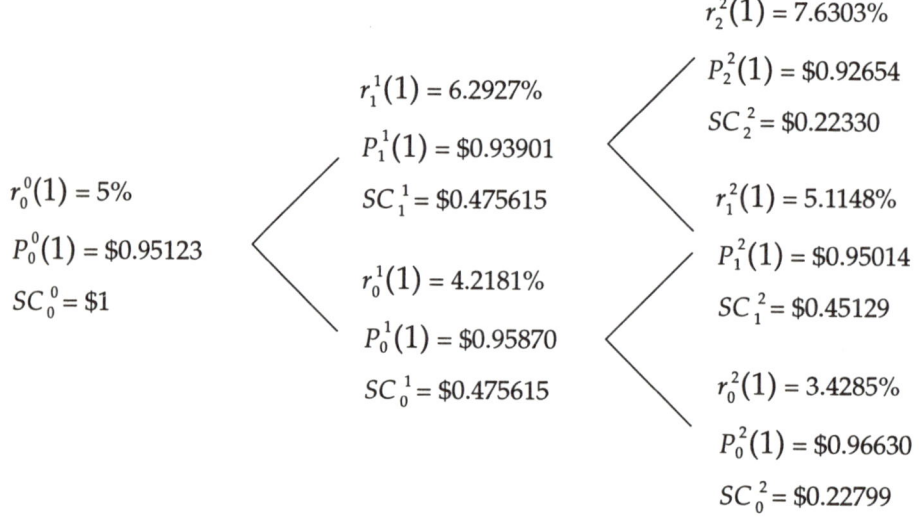

Recall that the value of a swap depends on the market forward rates and not on volatility. Hence, the interest rate model used to incorporate volatility should leave the value of the swap unchanged. The value attributed to volatility in the cap market is priced such that it equals the value attributed to volatility in the floor market. Therefore, all of the interest rate models developed here will yield the same equilibrium swap rates.

The Black, Derman, and Toy Model. Black, Derman, and Toy (1990) adopted a lognormal distribution that allows explicitly for time-varying rate volatility. Specifically, the stochastic differential equation can be expressed as

$dr = \mu(t)\,r\,dt + \sigma(t)\,r\,dz,$

where t allows for these parameters to be different across the term structure. Hence, the current term structure of volatilities, $\sigma(t)$, and the current term structure of interest rates, $\mu(t)$, are taken as inputs. This increased flexibility has made this model popular. We used this model when we explicitly evaluated the risk premium.

With time-varying volatilities, the binomial tree does not naturally recombine. Hence, care must be taken to force it to do so. Three observations are made to recombine the tree (assuming $q = 1/2$). First, the current zero-coupon bond prices must be obtained. Second, the volatility at each node at the same point in time must be the same; that is, the model assumes time-varying but not state-varying volatility. Third, the current term structure of volatility is given. With these three observations, the tree can be made to recombine and satisfy the original inputs.

The up- and down-jumps, respectively, are expressed as

$$r_{i+1}^{t+1}(1) = r_i^t(1)\,\exp[\mu^t(ts) + \sigma^t\sqrt{ts}\,]$$

and

$$r_i^{t+1}(1) = r_i^t(1)\,\exp[\mu^t(ts) - \sigma^t\sqrt{ts}\,],$$

where the t superscript denotes time. Time-varying volatility offers no assurance that the middle node at $t = 2$ will recombine. To force this result (to avoid an exploding tree), we allowed for different drift rates in the two subtrees emanating out of Time 1. We could construct the tree by jointly solving for the two drift rates and requiring the middle node to recombine. We assumed σ^1 equals 20 percent and σ^2 equals 18 percent.

The first-year drift term is 2.99463 percent, and the second-year drift terms are −2.03431 percent (up) and 1.96569 percent (down). Note that the expected future spot rates under the risk-neutral probability measure are 5.2554 percent and 5.3189 percent, respectively.[11] The expected one-period spot prices are $0.948854 and $0.94829, respectively. Figure 4 illustrates the first three points in time ($t = 0,1,2$) based on the Black, Derman, and Toy model.

Again, the cap equals the floor when the strike rate equals the equilibrium swap rate; that is,

$$
\begin{aligned}
CAP(5.3145\%,\ 3\text{-year}) &= 0.475615\,(0.93901)\,(0.064949 - 0.053145)\ (\text{Time 1, State 1})\\
&\quad + 0.22330\,(0.92884)\,(0.076613 - 0.053145)\ (\text{Time 2, State 2})\\
&= 0.005272 + 0.004867\\
&= 1.0139\%\ \text{of } NP,
\end{aligned}
$$

---

[11] 5.2554% = 0.50(6.2927%) + 0.50(4.2181%), and 5.3189% = 0.25(7.3820%) + 0.50(5.1502%) + 0.25(3.5932%).

and

FLR(5.3145%, 3-year) = $1.0(0.951229) (0.053145 – 0.051271) (Time 0, State 0)
$\qquad$ + 0.475615(0.95870) (0.053145 – 0.043083) (Time 1, State 0)
$\qquad$ + 0.22799(0.96471) (0.053145 – 0.036585) (Time 2, State 0)
$\qquad$ + 0.45129(0.94980) (0.053145 – 0.052851) (Time 2, State 1)
$\qquad$ = 0.001783 + 0.004588 + 0.003642 + 0.000126
$\qquad$ = 1.0139% of *NP*.

Figure 4.   Binomial Lattice: Black, Derman, and Toy Model

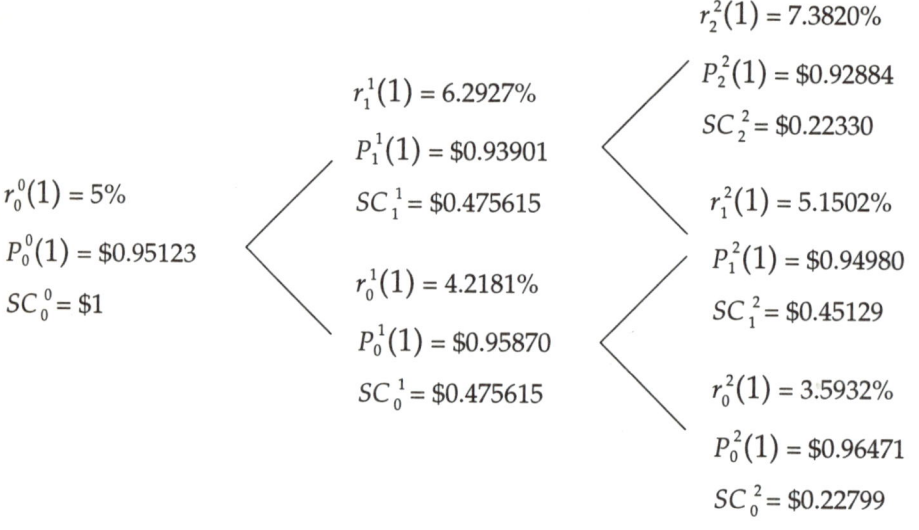

The Black and Karasinski Model. Black and Karasinski (1991) extended the work of Black, Derman, and Toy by explicitly incorporating a mean-reversion parameter, κ. Black, Derman, and Toy took the term structure of interest rates and the term structure of volatilities as observable values. Black and Karasinski also took these values as observables, but they needed one additional value to parameterize the mean-reversion parameter. They assumed the availability of a complete set of at-the-money caps. The stochastic differential equation can be expressed as

$$dr \;=\; \kappa(t)\{\ln[\mu(t)] - \ln[r(t)]\}rdt + \sigma(t)rdz.$$

Once again, care must be taken to assure that the binomial tree recombines. One way to accomplish this recombination is to allow the time step to vary. That is, the time step is selected to satisfy the restriction on kappa as well as to assure that up-then-down leads to the same place as down-then-up.

The up- and down-jumps, respectively, are as follows:

$$r_{i+1}^{t+1}(1) = r_i^t(1)\exp\{\kappa^t[\ln(\mu^t) - \ln(r^t)](ts) + \sigma^t\sqrt{ts}\}$$

and

$$r_i^{t+1}(1) = r_i^t(1)\exp\{\kappa^t[\ln(\mu^t) - \ln(r^t)](ts) - \sigma^t\sqrt{ts}\}.$$

The Hull and White Model. Hull and White (1996) demonstrated that their general framework is widely applicable. Their trinomial tree is similar to the binomial tree except the trinomial version has three arcs at each node. Their general stochastic differential equation is (where x could be r or any other factor)

$$dx = a\left[\frac{\theta(t)}{a} - x\right] dt + \sigma dz.$$

If x equals $\log(r)$, a equals $a(t)$, and σ equals $\sigma(t)$, we have the Black and Karasinski model. If x equals $\log(r)$ and $a(t)$ equals $-\sigma'(t)/\sigma(t)$, then we have the Black, Derman, and Toy model.

The choice of probability of up-, middle-, and down-jumps is constrained to be related to the size of the jumps. Hull and White adopted a method that keeps all the vertical distances between each node equal. (For more details, see Hull and White and references therein.)

The Heath, Jarrow, and Morton Model. The Heath, Jarrow, and Morton (1992) model allows each forward rate to change based on its own sensitivities to the underlying factors. Thus, the term structure can twist and turn in a wide variety of ways. The initial inputs consist of forward rates and forward rate volatilities. With these inputs correctly specified, one can derive the appropriate spot rate process, as well as the stochastic process, for bond prices. The stochastic differential equation of the family of forward rates can be expressed as

$$df(T) = \int_0^t \mu(v, T, \omega)dv + \sum_{i=1}^n \int_0^t \sigma_i(v, T, \omega)dW_i(v).$$

The level of complexity is clearly related to the number of factors required to appropriately specify the stochastic behavior of the term structure. (For further explanation of the details, see Jarrow 1996.)

The Ritchken and Sankarasubramanian Model. By transforming the Heath, Jarrow, and Morton spot rate process, Ritchken and Sankarasubramanian (1995) and Li, Ritchken, and Sankarasubramanian (1995) demonstrated that the transformed process can be modeled with a binomial lattice. Hence, they were able to keep track of the entire term structure contained within a binomial lattice. By assuming the following functional form for volatility, the actual volatility curve cannot be fit exactly:

$$\sigma_j^i \ (j, j+1) = \sigma r_i^i (1)^\gamma e^{-\kappa j};$$

where γ is a power term on the spot rate governing the sensitivity of volatility to the spot rate level and κ is a constant that governs the exponential dampening of volatility across maturity. Ritchken and Sankarasubramanian showed that the spot rate process is given by

$$dr = \mu(r, \phi, t) \ dt + \sigma r^t(1)^\gamma dw(t),$$

where

$$\mu(r, \phi, t) = \kappa[f^0(t) - r^t(1)] + \frac{\partial f^0(t)}{\partial t} + \phi(t),$$

and

$$d\phi(t) = \{\sigma^2[r^t(1)]^{2\gamma} - 2\kappa\phi(t)\}dt,$$

where $f^0(t)$ is the value of a forward rate starting at t and observed at $t = 0$ and the other variables are as previously defined. (For more details on implementing this model, see Ritchken 1996.)

Pricing versus Applying Interest Rate Swaps. Our empirical research focuses primarily on the consequences of using interest rate swaps rather than on pricing them, but the way interest rate swaps are priced is directly linked to whether they are applied in a particular circumstance. Interest rate swaps are usually explained following three steps. Campbell and Kracaw (1993) defined the procedure as follows:

Step 1. Determine the best guess of the floating rate applicable to each future settlement date in the swap.

Step 2. Use the zero-coupon yield curve to calculate the present value of the expected future floating-rate payments under the swap.

Step 3. Calculate the annuity that has the same present value as determined in Step 2.

The most difficult task in interest rate swap valuation is Step 1, determining the appropriate values related to the future floating-rate cash flows. Campbell and Kracaw explained,

. . . we know that the market's best guess of these rates (the floating rates) is embedded in long-term rates or in the yield curve. Hence, we can turn to the yield curve and extract the implied forward rates for each settlement date. We know . . . that the forward rate contains the market's best guess of the future spot rate, though it may also contain a liquidity premium.

To further delineate this general approach to valuing interest rate swaps, Dattatreya (1992) stated,

> . . . as far as valuation is concerned, we are indifferent between the unknown floating-rate cash flows or the known cash flows represented by forward rates. Once the floating side has been so "fixed," its present value is first computed simply by discounting each flow to the present. The swap rate can then be easily computed by determining that fixed-rate which will have the same discounted present value as the floating side.

The key phrase here is "as far as valuation is concerned." Dealers in forward rate agreements (FRAs)—the building blocks to valuing swaps—know that the cost to hedge a particular future floating-rate exposure is the current forward rate. The main focus of our research, therefore, is on the behavior of FRAs. Specifically, are there theoretical reasons that FRAs can deviate substantially from the expected future spot rate? If potential deviations exist, what has been their magnitude historically? Obviously, large deviations of FRA rates from the expected future spot rate will result in interest rate swaps, on average, having a nonzero expected return.

Two different costs are related to interest rate swaps. The first cost is the deviation of the market FRA rate from the expected spot rate. Considerable evidence suggests that, in fact, market FRA rates deviate, at least at times, from the expected spot rate. For example, Ho (1995) observed that

> . . . during 1993, the yield curve was historically steep (positively sloped). As a result, forward rates rose rapidly with maturity. Many investment professionals attributed the steepness of the curve to a significant imbalance of supply and demand in the bond market, and they, therefore, viewed the forward rates as very poor predictors of the rates that would be realized in the future.

Because interest rate swaps are valued based on arbitrage with FRAs, if the above observation is true, then in 1993, receive-fixed interest rate swaps offered significant return opportunities and receive-floating interest rate swaps would prove very costly. That is, in 1993, a speculator could have profited tremendously by just entering a receive-fixed interest rate swap (of course, short-term interest rates did run up in 1994).

The second cost related to interest rate swaps is the deviation of the investor's view from the FRA. That is, the current FRA fixed rate may be 8.0 percent, but the investor believes this rate will subsequently be 6.0 percent. Thus, the FRA may be biased 50 basis points higher than the expected future spot rate of, say, 7.5 percent, but an investor would still bear the cost of 150 basis points in expected return by hedging a floating-rate exposure with an FRA. Ho expressed this second cost in the context of interest rate options as follows: ". . . when the forward curve differs from the investors' predicted rates, part of the cost of the interest rate option value is the 'hedge cost'."

Although this second cost is vitally important when using interest rate swaps, we focused only on the first cost, the cost of any bias in FRAs embedded in interest rate swaps.

The Risk Premium within the Term Structure of Interest Rates

The traditional methods for valuing interest rate contingent claims in a multiperiod, discrete-time setting involve replacing actual probabilities with "risk-neutral" or "pseudo" probabilities.[12] For our objectives, this step is extremely important, especially if a firm's aversion to interest rate risk is distinctly different from the one implied by market equilibrium.

For example, a life insurance company with long-maturity liabilities may actually *prefer* to invest in long-maturity assets, and overall market equilibrium results in longer maturity assets receiving a higher yield. Market equilibrium may result in a rising forward curve, even though interest rates are not expected to change, because of a risk premium. In this case, the risk premium is paid to investors willing to hold long-maturity, fixed-rate debt. Thus, even though no arbitrage exists under risk-neutral valuation, different market participants will have very clear preferences regarding their own particular strategy.

Building upon the Black, Derman, and Toy model, we assumed that the data for five years, presented in Table 2, are currently observable in the market (or are beliefs held by a market participant). Setting the drift terms so that the tree recombines, making sure that the sum of the state claims equals the initial zero-coupon bond price, and achieving the appropriate level of local volatility, we found the rate tree and related statistics shown in Table 3.[13] The subjective probability of an up-jump was derived so that the original expected rate would be matched. For example, assuming a 37.68996 percent chance of an up-jump in the first time step, produces

6.2927 (0.3768996) + 4.2181 (1 – 0.3768996) = 5.0 percent.

Thus, the subjective probabilities are applied to the risk-neutral rate tree. The important observation at this point is that nothing is logically inconsistent with expected rates deviating from either forward rates or expected rates under a risk-neutral probability measure. This rate tree permits calculation of the state claims shown in Table 4.

---

[12]See, for example, Jarrow (1996) or Ritchken (1996).

[13]Local volatility is $\ln[r_i^t(1)/r_{i-1}^t(1)]/2$.

Table 2. Hypothetical Five-Year Data

Maturity (years)	Inputs			Outputs		
	Expected Rate	Forward Rate	Volatility	Zero-Coupon Price	Forward Price	Swap Rate
0	5.0%	5.00%	0.0%	—	—	—
1	5.0	5.25	20.0	$0.951229	$0.951229	5.12711%
2	5.0	5.30	18.0	0.902578	0.948854	5.25523
3	5.0	5.33	17.0	0.855987	0.948380	5.31453
4	5.0	5.35	16.0	0.811558	0.948096	5.35142
5				0.769280	0.947906	5.37729

Table 3. Hypothetical Rate Tree and Related Statistics by Time Point

State	0	1	2	3	4
0	5.0000%	6.2927%	7.3820%	8.5637%	9.7571%
1		4.2181	5.1502	6.0954	7.0851
2			3.5932	4.3385	5.1449
3				3.0880	3.7359
4					2.7129
Probability of up-jump	37.68996	45.26836	46.21416	46.08812	
Expected rates					
Subjective	5.0000	5.0000	5.0000	5.0000	5.0000
Risk-neutral	5.0000	5.2554	5.3189	5.3692	5.4140

Table 4. Hypothetical State Claims by Time Point

State	0	1	2	3	4
0	$1.00000	$0.47561	$0.22330	$0.10371	$0.04760
1		0.47561	0.45129	0.31802	0.19721
2			0.22799	0.32429	0.30487
3				0.10997	0.20857
4					0.05331
Sum	$1.00000	0.95123	0.90258	0.85599	0.81156

By design, the sum of the state claims equals the zero-coupon bond price. To consider the impact of a risk premium, we examined the cash flows from a receive-fixed, pay-floating, five-year interest rate swap. From Table 2, the equilibrium five-year swap rate is 5.37729 percent (discretely compounded). Table 5 gives the actual cash flows (discounted one period because we assume settlement in arrears) from this swap for each state at each point in time assuming annual resets and $1 million in notional principal.

Table 5. Hypothetical Cash Flows by Time Point

State	0	1	2	3	4
0	$2,379.80	$-10,494.19	$-21,214.51	$-32,712.67	$-44,188.42
1		10,248.15	875.07	-8,539.99	-18,304.83
2			16,581.01	9,032.53	928.72
3				21,729.55	15,130.89
4					25,569.91

For example, the single-period rate at t = 0 is 5.12711 percent (discrete). The swap pays the difference between the swap rate and the single-period rate settled in arrears. Thus, the difference (5.37729% – 5.12711%) must be discounted based on the current one-period bond price of $0.951229. Because we assume $1 million notional principal, we have

$1,000,000 ($0.1951229) (0.0537729 – 0.0512711) = $2,379.80.

A brief glance at the hypothetical cash flows may lead to the conclusion that, in fact, interest rate swaps are "fair" in the sense that sometimes you lose and sometimes you win. This analysis, however, quickly changes once you consider the subjective probabilities of each outcome. Table 6 gives both the subjective probabilities and the risk-neutral probabilities. For each case, the expected cash flows for each point in time are computed along with the sum of the expected cash flows.

Table 6. Hypothetical Cash Flows and Expected Cash Flows by Time Point

State	0	1	2	3	4
Subjective probabilities					
0	100.0000%	37.6900%	17.0616%	7.8849%	3.6340%
1		62.3100	48.8351	31.7455	18.8818
2			34.1033	42.0269	36.4840
3				18.3428	31.1113
4					9.8889
Risk-neutral probabilities					
0	100.0000	50.0000	25.0000	12.5000	6.2500
1		50.0000	50.0000	37.5000	25.0000
2			25.0000	37.5000	37.5000
3				12.5000	25.0000
4					6.2500
Expected cash flows from five–year swap					
Subjective	$2,379.80	$2,430.37	$2,462.47	$2,491.48	$2,512.76
Risk-neutral	2,379.80	-123.02	-720.84	-1,188.19	-1,608.87

Table 6 is extremely revealing. For example, consider a firm that will soon issue either floating-rate debt or five-year, fixed-rate debt. The realization that issuing fixed-rate debt will cost, on average per year, 23–25 basis points more than issuing floating-rate debt may alter the firm's decision. In this context, understanding how higher rates affect the firm is important. For example, if the firm has a low debt-to-asset ratio, a strong profit margin, and sales that are not sensitive to interest rates, then 25 basis points may be too much to pay to fix its interest cost for five years. A highly leveraged, rate-sensitive firm, however, may prefer to lock in the fixed rate despite the premium.

The Empirical Evidence

The magnitude of the risk premium within the existing term structure of interest rates is an empirical issue. We examined historical data on the Eurodollar cash and futures markets. LIBOR has emerged as the interest rate of choice among swap dealers, largely because of its close relationship to the dealers' cost of funds and its high level of liquidity. The EDF markets are a good proxy for forward rates for short-maturity contracts.

The primary data cover the period October 21, 1986, to March 29, 1996, with daily observations on three-month LIBOR and the first eight 90-day EDF contract settle prices. The data also include monthly observations on the (all urban, not seasonally adjusted) consumer price index (CPI).

Figure 5 illustrates cash LIBOR and a one-year moving average of the CPI for the entire sample period. LIBOR started and ended this period at about 6 percent. The latter part of the 1980s exhibited higher and more volatile rates than did the early 1990s. The highest rate during this period was 10.625 percent on March 21, 1989, and the lowest rate was 3.125 percent on October 2, 1992.

Although inflation and interest rates are clearly related, they are far from perfectly correlated: The correlation coefficient for this period was 0.66. Of course, interest rates are forward looking, whereas inflation rates are historical. The average three-month LIBOR rate was 6.27 percent with a standard deviation of 32 percent (annualized), and the average CPI percentage change was 3.65 percent with a standard deviation of 17.7 percent (annualized).

Eurodollar Futures and Interest Rate Swaps. One result of the marking-to-market feature of EDFs is that the implied futures rate deviates from the forward rate. Because our primary data are on EDFs and our focus is interest rate swaps, we examined the magnitude of this difference. Burghardt and Hoskins (1994, 1995a, 1995b) and Meulbroek (1992), among others, have studied this financing bias (the EDF gains are invested and losses

**Figure 5.   Cash Three-Month LIBOR and Percentage Change in the
              Consumer Price Index, October 21, 1986, to March 29, 1996**

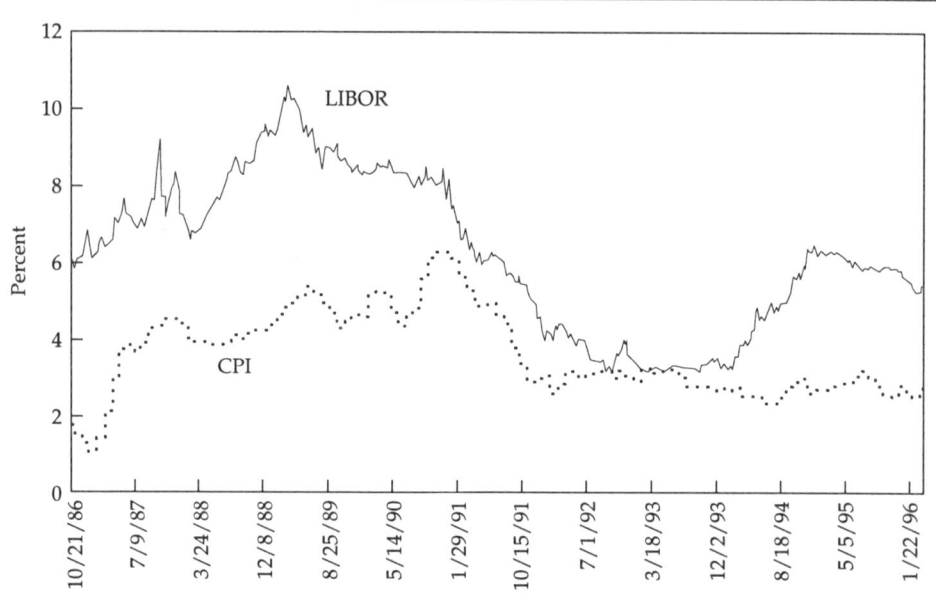

must be financed because of the daily mark to market) or the convexity bias (interest rate swap values have a convex relationship to interest rates because they are not marked to market). Changes in interest rates have the same effect on interest rate swaps as they do on regular bonds; that effect is negative with positive convexity. The relationship between interest rates and EDFs is linear, $25.00 per basis point per contract.

Our objective was not to reassess this bias but to evaluate its effect. Although Burghardt and Hoskins (1995a) asserted that "the bias can be huge," they focused on long-dated interest rate swaps. For two-year swap rates, the convexity bias accounts for approximately 3 basis points in the swap rate, and for an individual forward rate agreement, the convexity bias is approximately 1 basis point. The empirical evidence indicates that the historical premium in two-year swap rates has been roughly 50 basis points. We used EDF data because of its high liquidity and precision, but we chose to ignore the convexity bias because it is a relatively minor factor for the issue we addressed. Also, when market participants became aware of this bias is unclear.

Illustrations of the Risk Premium. We illustrate here the relationship between cash LIBOR and the rate implied by an EDF (sometimes called the basis) over a two-year period. We selected two time periods: one when LIBOR rates were rising (June 1993 to June 1995) and one when rates were falling (June 1991 to June 1993).

Figure 6 is particularly interesting because of the behavior of the EDF. Between June 1993 and June 1995, cash LIBOR rose from the low 3 percent range to the 6 percent range. The unbiased expectations hypothesis would assert that an unbiased forecast of the three-month LIBOR rate in June 1995 would be the forward rate implied in the 6/95 EDF contract observed in June 1993. We might be tempted to argue that in June 1993, the 6/95 EDF was a fairly good predictor of three-month LIBOR in June 1995. During this two-year period, the estimates were at times too low and at other times too high, but on average, the forecasts were fairly accurate, which is not usually the case. An alternative explanation would be that rates rose higher than expected so the risk premium was dissipating. The convergence of the futures rate to cash LIBOR is rapid during the last 90 days of the contract. Hence, we argue that the EDF rate two years out contains at least two major factors: the market's forecast of rates and a risk premium.

Figure 6.   Illustration of Basis, June 1993 to June 1995

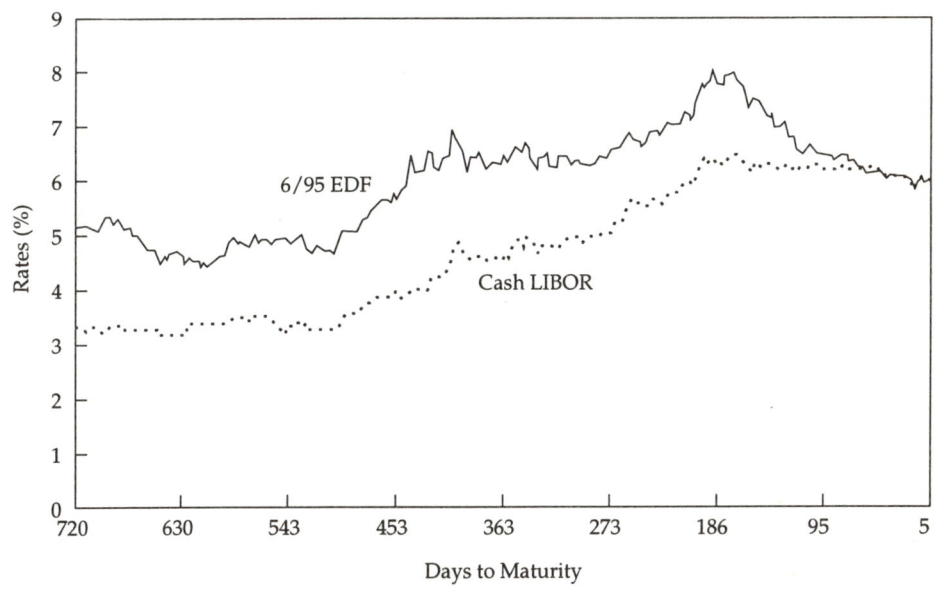

Figure 7 illustrates the same phenomenon for June 1991 to June 1993 except that cash LIBOR rates were generally falling. In June 1991, an unbiased forecast of LIBOR in June 1993 was 8.5 percent. Figure 7 illustrates the typical pattern of a dissipating risk premium.

Figure 7.   Illustration of Basis, June 1991 to June 1993

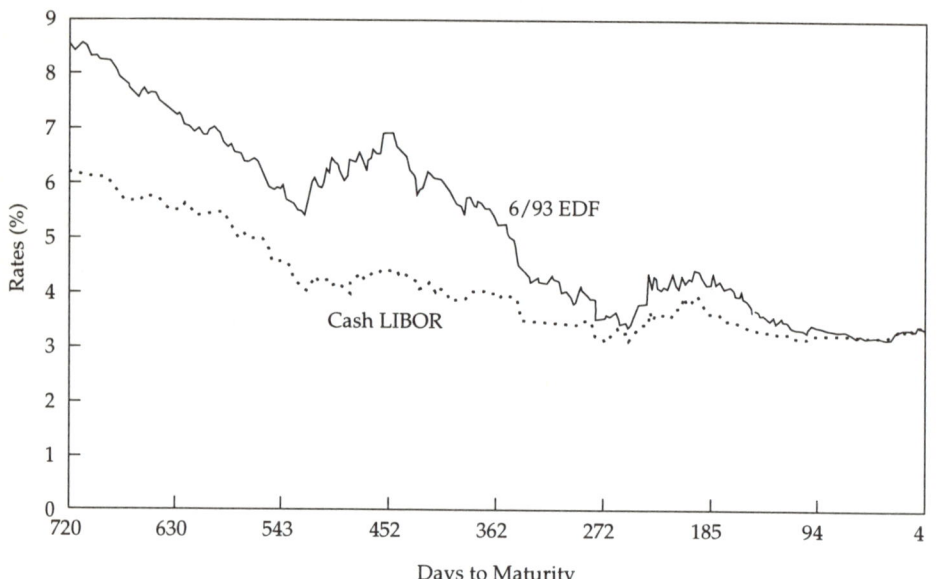

Analysis of Overall Period. This section presents an analysis of the average forward rate implied by the EDF data, rate volatility and related factors, the swap premium, and the behavior of the basis average by weeks to maturity. The period of observation is October 21, 1986, to March 29, 1996.

The data consist of the daily cash LIBOR rates and settle prices for eight EDFs. For the "nearby" EDF (closest to maturity on the observation date), the days to maturity range anywhere from 1 day to about 92 days. Hence, the nearby EDF rate is observed, on average, one-half a quarter (46 days) from maturity.

Figure 8 illustrates the average rates implied by the eight EDF contracts during the entire study period. The average forward rates start at 6.3 percent for the nearby contract and rise monotonically to 7.6 percent for the eighth contract. In terms of historical forward rates, the difference between the nearby contract and the two-year contract has been 130 basis points.

The difference between rates is 13 basis points between the first and second contracts, 19 basis points between the second and third, 23 basis points between the fourth and fifth, and 15 basis points for the seventh and eighth

Figure 8.   Average Quarterly Forward Curve, October 21, 1986, to March 29, 1996

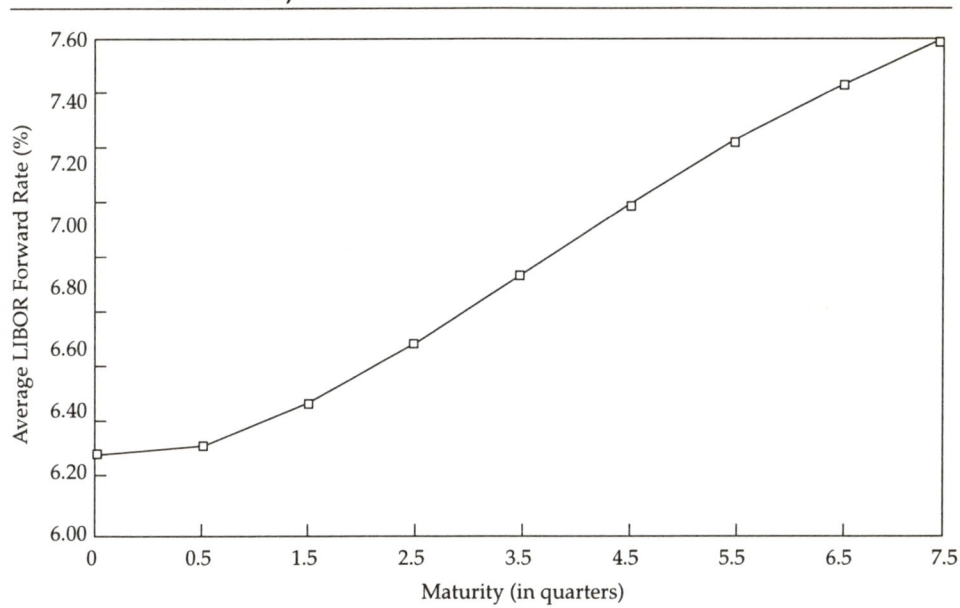

contracts. A standard one-tailed *t*-test indicates that each nearby pair of quarterly bases is statistically different at the 1 percent level, which is strong evidence in favor of a significantly positive basis. Thus, the risk premium clearly is a function of maturity.

Figure 9 illustrates the behavior of the annualized standard deviation in percentage (volatility) of these eight EDF contracts and cash LIBOR.[14] The volatility is clearly a declining function of maturity. Also, the relationship appears to be nonlinear. Hence, the leveling out of volatility is consistent with the leveling out of the average forward rates.

To isolate the factors leading to declining volatility, we considered the following representation of the *i*th forward rate:

$$f_t = f_0 + \sum_{j=1}^{i} (f_j - f_{j-1}) = f_0 + \sum_{j=1}^{i} s_j,$$

where f_0 is cash LIBOR and s denotes the difference between nearby forward rates, or a spread. The *i*th forward rate can be viewed as cash LIBOR plus the

---

[14]The daily standard deviation was computed and multiplied by the square root of 252, the annual number of trading days.

Figure 9. Volatility of Forward Curve, October 21, 1986, to March 29, 1996

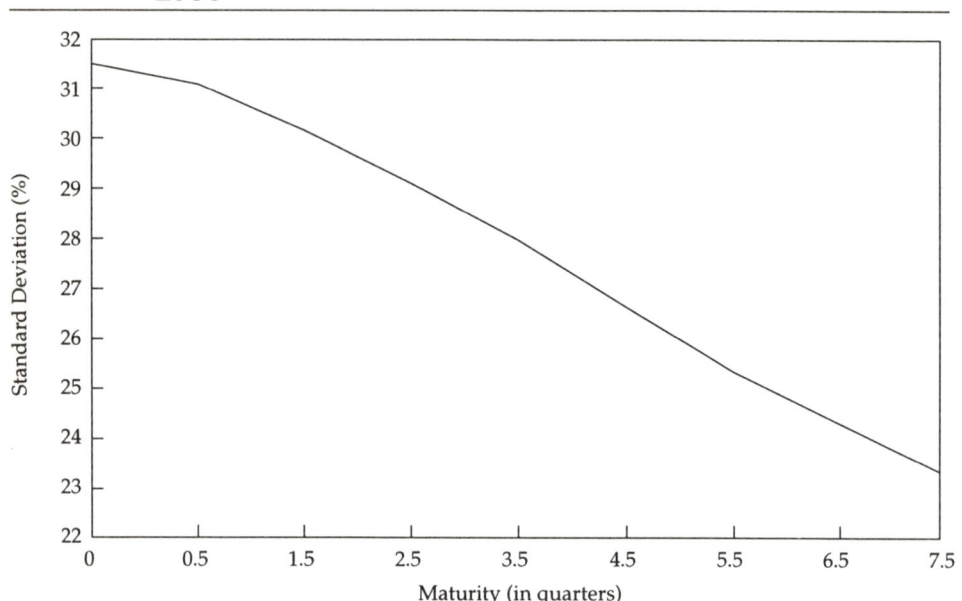

incremental spread between forward rates moving out on the term structure. Thus, the variance of the ith forward rate can be expressed as

$$\sigma^2_{f_i} = \sigma^2_{f_0} + \sum_{j=1}^{i}\sigma^2_{s_j} + 2\sigma_{f_0}\sum_{j=1}^{i}\sigma_{s_j}\rho_{f_0,s_j} + 2\sum_{i=1}^{i-1}\sum_{j=i+1}^{i}\sigma_{s_i}\sigma_{s_j}\rho_{s_i,s_j},$$

where $\sigma^2_{f_0}$ denotes the variance of cash LIBOR, σ is the standard deviation, and ρ is the relevant correlations.

Table 7 provides the statistics necessary to decompose the variance of the ith forward rate into its component parts. The average spread rises and then falls. The standard deviation peaks at Quarter 2 and monotonically declines thereafter. Also, the spreads are not highly correlated. Hence, the more-distant forward rates are less volatile than the nearer rates, partly because of this portfolio effect. That is, the forward rate can be viewed as a portfolio of cash LIBOR and spreads. The negative correlation between cash LIBOR and the spread is intuitive; when interest rates are high, on average, the term structure is flatter (perhaps because participants expect rates to fall).

Table 7.   Statistics on LIBOR and Quarterly Spread (First Difference) on the Basis, October 21, 1986, to March 29, 1996

	LIBOR	1	2	3	4	5	6	7	8
Average	6.265%	0.031%	0.139%	0.188%	0.216%	0.226%	0.203%	0.174%	0.152%
Standard deviation	31.58	3.36	4.71	3.24	2.57	2.59	2.47	2.19	2.08
Correlations									
LIBOR	1.00	−0.20	−0.33	−0.48	−0.57	−0.60	−0.63	−0.59	−0.59
1		1.00	0.60	0.43	0.15	0.01	−0.05	−0.03	−0.10
2			1.00	0.63	0.44	0.12	0.27	−0.004	0.04
3				1.00	0.52	0.47	0.29	0.57	0.13
4					1.00	0.57	0.60	0.41	0.73
5						1.00	0.62	0.66	0.48
6							1.00	0.60	0.68
7								1.00	0.58
8									1.00

To understand how rising forward rates affect swap rates, we estimated the swap curve based on the average forward rates. We approximated the quarterly forward rates by linear interpolation. Table 8 presents the results of this analysis. The second column presents average quarterly forward rates based on this data set. The first quarter was based on the average cash LIBOR rate. We assumed that the nearest EDF was, on average, one-half of a quarter from maturity and that the second nearest EDF was one and a half quarters from maturity. Using linear interpolation, we computed the average forward rate for a one-quarter maturity contract. The third column presents the swap rates using the same valuation approach described earlier. The fourth column presents the swap premium measured as the difference between the swap rate and the average LIBOR rate (Quarter 1 forward rate of 6.27 percent). The fifth column lists the annual savings from entering a receive-fixed and pay-floating interest rate swap per $1 million notional principal (which translates into $100.00 times the swap premium).[15] A rising forward curve translates directly into a rising swap curve. With a consistently rising swap curve, swaps are a nonzero average payoff transaction when a risk premium exists.

For example, consider a large corporation that will maintain the duration of its liabilities either at about three months or at two years. The longer-duration strategy provides more stability for the firm, but it is costly in the long run. Table 8 shows that the average cost is 57.6 basis points, or $5,760.00 per $1 million. Instead of locking in 6.84 percent for the two years (via the

---

[15]The numbers are slightly different because of rounding of the swap premium.

swap), the corporation could have paid an average of 6.27 percent for this period. Historically, firms would have been much better off by issuing floating-rate debt as opposed to fixed-rate debt if the debt could have been issued at a constant spread to LIBOR. This conclusion obviously assumes that interest rates cannot be forecast and that issuance costs are approximately the same for each type of debt.

Table 8.   Swap Curve Derived from Average Futures Rates, October 21, 1986, to March 29, 1996

Quarter	Forward Rate	Swap Rate	Swap Premium (basis points)	$ Savings ($1 million/year)
1	6.27%	6.27%	0.0	$ 0
2	6.53	6.32	4.8	483
3	6.73	6.39	11.8	1,179
4	6.95	6.47	20.3	2,026
5	7.17	6.56	29.6	2,955
6	7.35	6.66	39.2	3,915
7	7.52	6.75	48.6	4,856
8	7.67	6.84	57.6	5,760

To understand the risk premium (futures rate minus the expected spot rate) better, we examined the basis (futures rate minus the current spot rate) on a weekly basis. On any given day, if the nearest EDF contract matures in less than 7 days, all eight EDFs are classified as being in the first week; if it matures in less than 14 days (but more than 7 days), then they are in the second week. Figure 10 illustrates the average basis for the 13 weeks in a quarter for the eight contracts—from the nearest contract at the bottom of the graph to the farthest at the top. Notice that the basis increases from Week 1 to Week 13. The nearest contract has an average of 10 basis points in the 13th week; the second nearest has 30 basis points, a difference of 20 basis points. The difference between the seventh and eighth contracts is only 12 basis points in the 13th week. Figure 10 provides strong evidence of a dissipating risk premium, although the rate of dissipation is not constant.

Figure 11 illustrates the standard deviation of the basis by week to maturity. The standard deviation and the average basis are clearly directly related. The rapid increase in the basis for the nearby contract corresponds to a rapid increase in standard deviation. This observation supports the notion that the risk premium is related to the corresponding risk.

Figure 12 illustrates the positive relationship between the average basis and the standard deviation of the basis. For the longer maturities, the results are clustered based on the specific quarterly contract. Figure 12 presents strong evidence that the basis is, in fact, compensation for risk bearing, if risk is measured as the standard deviation.

Figure 10. Average Weekly Basis for Eight EDF Contracts, October 21, 1986, to March 29, 1996

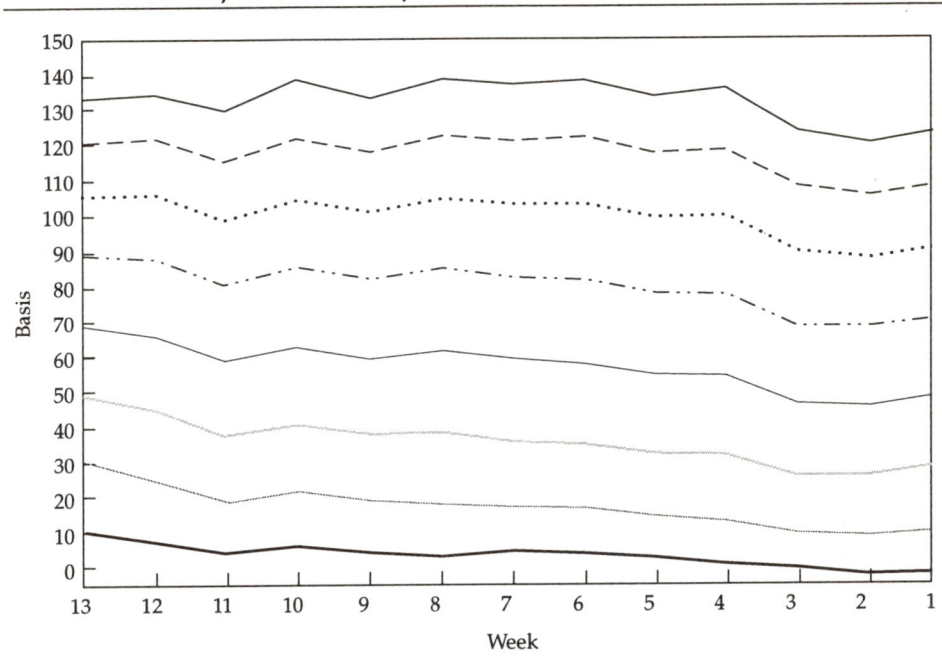

Analysis of Subperiods. Figure 13 illustrates the average daily basis by year (excluding partial years 1996 and 1986), again with the nearest contract on the bottom. With the exception of 1989 and 1990, the pattern consistently shows an increasing basis for longer maturity EDF contracts. In the years 1989 and 1990, rates initially were relatively high but fell sharply over the year. Figure 13 provides strong support for the assertion that a receive-fixed, pay-floating interest rate swap is a positive-dollar-return proposition.

Figure 14 illustrates the standard deviation of the basis by year. This pattern is much less consistent than that for the basis itself. For the whole period, the standard deviation is monotonically increasing, but for many years, this relationship does not hold.

Table 9 helps interpret the information contained in Figures 13 and 14. This table provides some statistics, including the R^2 of a time-series regression, by year, for cash LIBOR. For example, in 1994, cash LIBOR rose from 3.4 percent at the beginning of the year to 6.5 percent at the end of the year. An R^2 of 0.92 suggests that the trend was nearly linear—92 percent of the variation is explained by time. A glance back at Figure 5 confirms this result.

**Figure 11. Standard Deviation of Weekly Basis for Eight EDF
Contracts, October 21, 1986, to March 29, 1996**

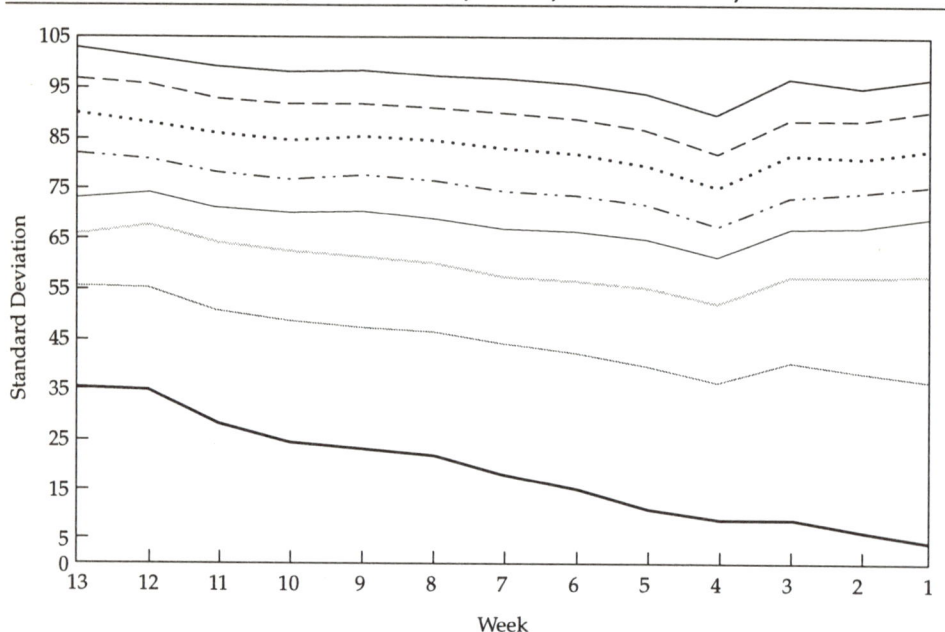

As Figure 13 shows, even in a strongly rising interest rate market, such as 1994, the average basis is monotonically increasing. In 1993, the market was trendless (R^2 of 0.23 in Table 9), yet the basis is still monotonically increasing. In 1992, the interest rate market fell sharply and had more volatility than the rising market of 1994; the basis is also monotonically increasing. The rising markets of 1987 and 1988 also record the consistently increasing basis.

Table 10 examines the average basis by calendar month. The average basis is the lowest in the last three months of the year and the highest in January, March, and April. The largest month-to-month change in the average basis for the eighth EDF contract (eight quarters to maturity) is December to January, for which the average basis rises from 112 to 154. After April, the basis falls steadily until the end of the year.

Summary

This study addressed the return side of the decision to use either interest rate swaps or other interest rate contingent claims. On average, the receive-fixed interest rate swap resulted in net receipts during the sample period. The U.S. interest rate market offers a significant risk premium. Thus, the decision to use interest rate swaps has a direct consequence for expected return.

Figure 12. Analysis of Weekly Basis, October 21, 1986, to March 29, 1996

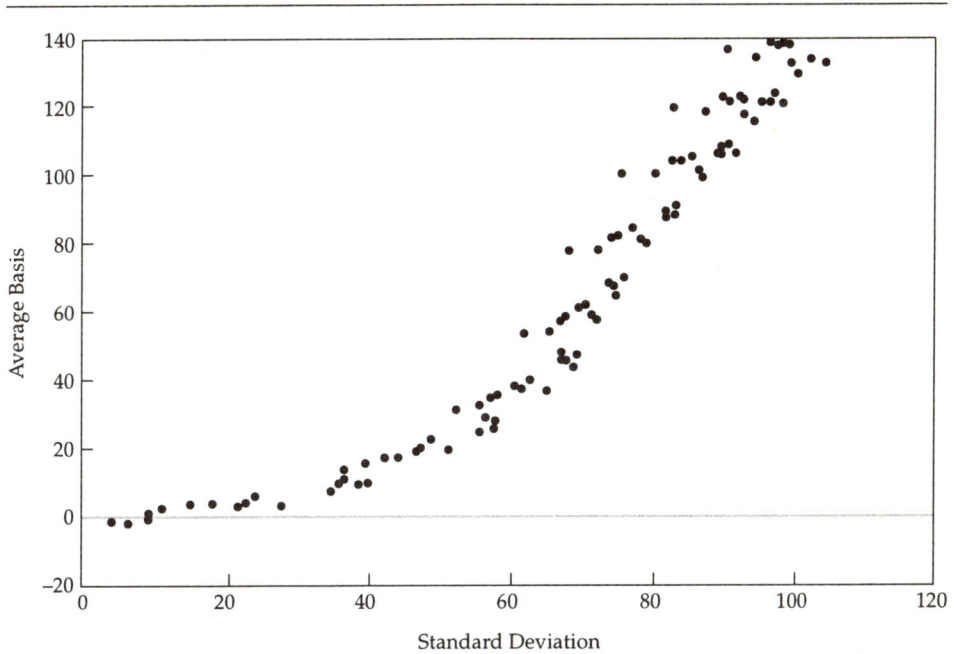

Using the Black, Derman, and Toy (1990) model, we illustrated theoretically the economic consequences of a risk premium. The risk premium is defined as the difference between the current forward rate and the expected future spot rate. Through a numerical example, we showed how an at-market swap with the existence of a risk premium can have a significant impact on the expected return from using the swap. The main insight is that whereas valuation is based on "risk-neutral," no-arbitrage relationships, expected returns are based on subjective probabilities (unadjusted for risk).

Considerable evidence favors a dissipating risk premium. The average forward rate implied in Eurodollar futures rises with maturity. Specifically, during this entire period, the difference between the shortest maturity contract and the two-year contract was 130 basis points. Second, the dissipating risk premium appears to be a nonlinear function of maturity, and most of the dissipation occurs between six months to one and a half years to maturity. This finding corresponds to anecdotal evidence of a humped forward volatility curve observed frequently in the cap-and-floor market. An analysis of subperiods reveals that these results are fairly consistent over time.

Figure 13. Average Daily Basis by Year

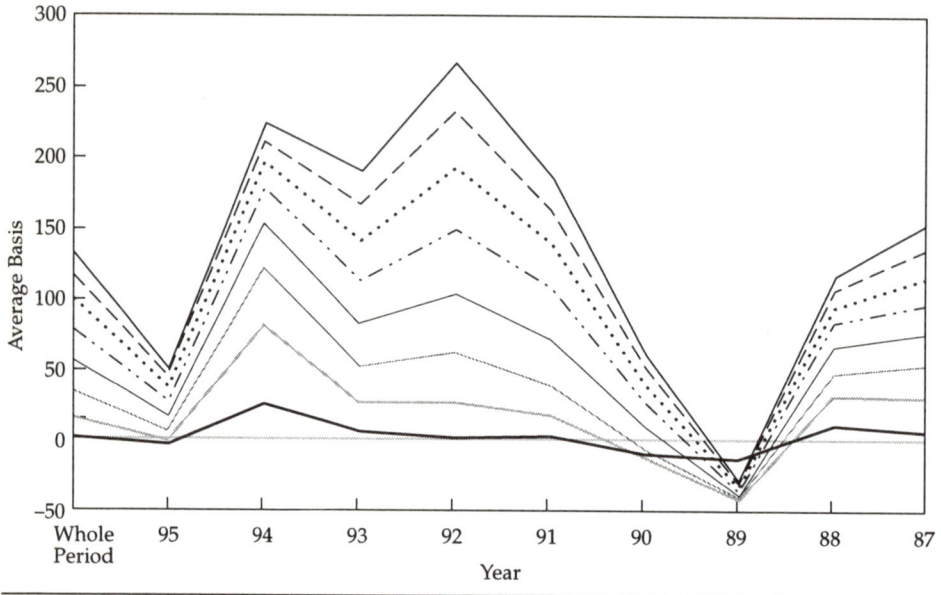

Figure 14. Standard Deviation of Basis by Year

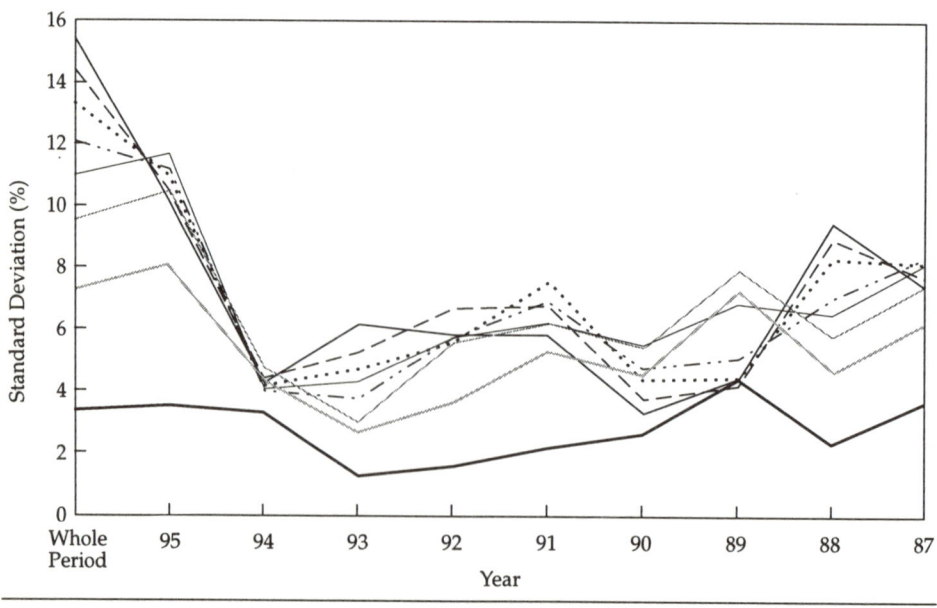

Table 9. Analysis of Cash LIBOR by Calendar Year

Year	Open	High	Low	Close	Average	Standard Deviation	High minus Low	Open minus Close	R^2
1987	6.3%	9.3%	6.1%	7.4%	7.2%	0.65%	3.2%	−1.1%	0.70
1988	7.4	9.6	6.6	9.3	8.0	0.84	3.0	−1.9	0.91
1989	9.3	10.6	8.3	8.4	9.3	0.60	2.3	0.9	0.65
1990	8.4	8.8	7.6	7.6	8.3	0.21	1.2	0.8	0.45
1991	7.6	7.7	4.3	4.3	6.0	0.72	3.4	3.3	0.91
1992	4.2	4.4	3.1	3.4	3.8	0.37	1.3	0.8	0.56
1993	3.4	3.5	3.2	3.4	3.3	0.09	0.3	0.1	0.23
1994	3.4	6.5	3.3	6.5	4.8	0.90	3.3	−3.1	0.92
1995	6.5	6.5	5.6	5.6	6.0	0.19	0.9	0.9	0.80
Average	6.3	7.4	5.3	6.2	6.3	0.5	2.1	0.1	0.70

Table 10. Average Monthly Basis by EDF Contract, January 1987 through December 1995

Month	1	2	3	4	5	6	7	8
January	6	23	45	77	90	112	130	154
February	5	21	41	72	86	107	126	149
March	14	35	61	80	96	115	135	148
April	15	39	72	85	107	126	150	157
May	5	28	60	73	96	117	141	147
June	3	25	46	62	85	107	123	133
July	2	28	35	58	81	110	119	136
August	1	25	31	54	79	110	120	135
September	7	21	34	56	84	104	116	131
October	−2	−4	15	38	71	81	98	112
November	−1	−11	8	31	63	75	95	110
December	−6	−3	15	40	63	77	94	112

References

Barclay, Michael J., and Clifford W. Smith, Jr. 1995. "The Maturity Structure of Corporate Debt." *Journal of Finance,* vol. 50, no. 2 (June):609–31.

Belton, Terry, and Galen Burghardt. 1990. "The Financing Bias in Eurodollar Futures Prices." Discount Corporation of New York Futures, March 22.

Black, Fischer, Emanuel Derman, and William Toy. 1990. "A One-Factor Model of Interest Rates and Its Application to Treasury Bond Options." *Financial Analysts Journal*, vol. 46, no. 1 (January/February):33–39.

Black, Fischer, and Piotr Karasinski. 1991. "Bond and Option Pricing When Short Rates Are Lognormal." *Financial Analysts Journal*, vol. 47, no. 4 (July/August):52–59.

Brennan, Michael J., and Eduardo S. Schwartz. 1977. "Savings Bonds, Retractable Bonds and Callable Bonds." *Journal of Financial Economics*, vol. 5, no. 1 (August):67–88.

———. 1979. "A Continuous Time Approach to the Pricing of Bonds." *Journal of Banking and Finance*, vol. 3, no. 2 (July):133–55.

Brooks, Robert, Myung J. Kim, and Miles Livingston. 1993. "The Unbiased Expectations Hypothesis and Error Learning." *Advances in Quantitative Analysis of Finance and Accounting*, vol. 2, part A:105–13.

Brooks, Robert, Haim Levy, and Miles Livingston. 1995. "Are Term Premiums Risk Premiums?" *Advances in Quantitative Analysis of Finance and Accounting*, vol. 3, part A:131–46.

Brown, Keith C., and Donald J. Smith. 1995. *Interest Rate and Currency Swaps: A Tutorial.* Charlottesville, VA: The Research Foundation of the Institute of Chartered Financial Analysts.

Burghardt, Galen, and Bill Hoskins. 1994. "The Convexity Bias in Eurodollar Futures." Research note, Dean Witter Institutional Futures (September 16).

———. 1995a. "The Convexity Bias in Eurodollar Futures: Part 1." *Derivatives Quarterly*, vol. 1, no. 3 (Spring):47–55.

———. 1995b. "A Question of Bias." *Risk*, vol. 8, no. 3 (March): 63–70.

Campbell, Tim S., and William A. Kracaw. 1993. *Financial Risk Management: Fixed Income and Foreign Exchange.* New York: HarperCollins College Publishers.

Courtadon, Georges. 1982. "The Pricing of Options on Default-Free Bonds." *Journal of Financial and Quantitative Analysis*, vol. 17, no. 1 (March):75–100.

Cox, John C., Jonathan E. Ingersoll, Jr., and Stephen A. Ross. 1981. "A Re-Examination of Traditional Hypotheses about the Term Structure of Interest Rates." *Journal of Finance*, vol. 36, no. 4 (September):769–99.

_____. 1985a. "An Intertemporal General Equilibrium Model of Asset Prices." *Econometrica*, vol. 53, no. 2 (March):363–84.

_____. 1985b. "A Theory of the Term Structure of Interest Rates." *Econometrica*, vol. 53, no. 2 (March):385–407.

Culbertson, J.M. 1957. "The Term Structure of Interest Rates." *Quarterly Journal of Economics*, vol. 71, no. 4 (November):485–517.

Dattatreya, Ravi E. 1992. "Interest Rate Swaps." *The 1992 Dictionary of Derivatives* (with June issue of *Euromoney*):31–35.

Dothan, L. Uri. 1978. "On the Term Structure of Interest Rates." *Journal of Financial Economics*, vol. 6, no. 1 (March):59–69.

Engle, Robert F., and Victor K. Ng. 1993. "Time-Varying Volatility and the Dynamic Behavior of the Term Structure." *Journal of Money, Credit, and Banking*, vol. 25 (August, part 1):336–49.

Fama, E.F. 1976a. "Forward Rates as Predictors of Future Spot Interest Rates." *Journal of Financial Economics*, vol. 3, no. 4 (October):361–77.

_____. 1976b. "Inflation Uncertainty and Expected Returns on Treasury Bills." *Journal of Political Economy*, vol. 84, no. 3 (June):427–48.

_____. 1984a. "The Information in the Term Structure." *Journal of Financial Economics*, vol. 13, no. 4 (December):509–28.

_____. 1984b. "Term Premiums in Bond Returns." Journal of Financial Economics, vol. 13, no. 4 (December):529–46.

Fisher, Irving. 1896. "Appreciation and Interest." *Publications of the American Economic Association*, vol. 11, no. 4 (August).

Goswami, Gautam, Thomas Noe, and Michael Rebello. 1995. "Debt Financing under Asymmetric Information." *Journal of Finance*, vol. 50, no. 2 (June):633–59.

Heath, D., R. Jarrow, and A. Morton. 1992. "Bond Pricing and the Term Structure of Interest Rates: A New Methodology." *Econometrica*, vol. 60, no. 1:77–105.

Hicks, J. R. 1946. *Value and Capital*, 2nd ed. London: Oxford University Press.

Ho, Thomas S.Y. 1995. "Evolution of Interest Rate Models: A Comparison." *Journal of Derivatives*, vol. 2, no. 4 (Summer):9–20.

Ho, Thomas S.Y., and Sang-Bin Lee. 1986. "Term Structure Movements and Pricing Interest Rate Contingent Claims." *Journal of Finance*, vol. 41, no. 5 (December):1011–29.

Hull, John, and Alan White. 1996. "Using Hull–White Interest Rate Trees." *Journal of Derivatives*, vol. 3, no. 3 (Spring):26–36.

Jarrow, Robert A. 1996. *Modelling Fixed Income Securities and Interest Rate Options*. New York: McGraw-Hill.

Langetieg, Terence C. 1980. "A Multivariate Model of the Term Structure." *Journal of Finance*, vol. 35, no. 1 (March):71–97.

Levy, Haim, and Robert Brooks. 1989. "An Empirical Analysis of Term Premiums Using Stochastic Dominance." *Journal of Banking and Finance*, vol. 13, no. 2 (May):245–60.

Li, Anlong, Peter Ritchken, and L. Sankarasubramanian. 1995. "Lattice Models for Pricing American Interest Rate Claims." *Journal of Finance*, vol. 50, no. 2 (June):719–37.

Longstaff, Francis A., and Eduardo S. Schwartz. 1992. "Interest Rate Volatility and the Term Structure: A Two-Factor General Equilibrium Model." *Journal of Finance*, vol. 47, no. 4 (September):1259–82.

Masulis, R. 1988. *The Debt/Equity Choice.* Cambridge, MA: Ballinger Publishing.

Meiselman, David. 1962. *The Term Structure of Interest Rates.* Englewood Cliffs, NJ: Prentice Hall.

Merton, R.C. 1974. "On the Pricing of Corporate Debt: The Risk Structure of Interest Rates." *Journal of Finance*, vol. 29, no. 2 (May): 449–70.

Meulbroek, Lisa. 1992. "A Comparison of Forward and Futures Prices of an Interest Rate-Sensitive Financial Asset." *Journal of Finance*, vol. 47, no. 1 (March):381–96.

Modigliani, F., and R. Sutch. 1966. "Innovations in Interest Rate Policy." *American Economic Review*, vol. 56, no. 2 (May):178–97.

Nawalkha, Sanjay K., and Donald R. Chambers. 1995. "The Binomial Model and Risk Neutrality: Some Important Details." *Financial Review*, vol. 30, no. 3 (August):605–15.

Rendleman, Richard J., and Brit J. Bartter. 1980. "The Pricing of Options on Debt Securities." *Journal of Financial and Quantitative Analysis*, vol. 15, no. 1 (March):11–24.

Richard, Scott F. 1978. "An Arbitrage Model of the Term Structure of Interest Rates." *Journal of Financial Economics*, vol. 6, no. 1 (March):33–57.

Ritchken, Peter. 1996. *Derivative Markets Theory, Strategy, and Applications.* New York: HarperCollins.

Ritchken, Peter, and L. Sankarasubramanian. 1995. "Volatility Structures of Forward Rates and the Dynamics of the Term Structure." *Mathematical Finance*, vol. 5, no.1 (January):55–72.

Sharpe, William F. 1995. "Nuclear Financial Economics." In William H. Beaver and George Parker, eds., *Risk Management Problems and Solutions.* New York: McGraw-Hill:17–35.

Tuckman, Bruce. 1995. *Fixed Income Securities Tools for Today's Markets.* New York: John Wiley & Sons.

Vasicek, Oldrich. 1977. "An Equilibrium Characterization of the Term Structure." *Journal of Financial Economics*, vol. 5, no. 2 (November):177–88.